Going Places

Yellowstone National Park

Cari Meister

ABDO Publishing Company

visit us at
www.abdopub.com

Published by ABDO Publishing Company 4940 Viking Drive, Edina, Minnesota 55435.
Copyright © 2000 by Abdo Consulting Group, Inc. International copyrights reserved in all countries. No part of this book may be reproduced in any form without written permission from the publisher.

Printed in the United States.

Photo credits: Peter Arnold, Inc.

Edited by Lori Kinstad Pupeza
Contributing editor Morgan Hughes
Graphic designs by Linda O'Leary

Library of Congress Cataloging-in-Publication Data

Meister, Cari.
      Yellowstone National Park / Cari Meister.
      p. cm. -- (Going Places)
      Includes index.
      Summary: Presents the geographic features, plant and animal life, and other attractions of the first national park.
      ISBN 1-57765-026-3
      1. Yellowstone National Park--Juvenile literature. [1. Yellowstone National Park. 2. National parks and reserves.] I. Title. II. Series: Meister, Cari. Going places.
      F722.M45 2000
      917.87'52--dc21

                                              98-10605
                                          CIP
                                          AC

Contents

Tall Tales 4

The First National Park 6

Glaciers and Volcanoes 8

Hot Springs and Mud Pots 10

Geysers 12

Wildlife 14

Plant Life 16

Fun Things to Do 18

Help Preserve Yellowstone 20

Glossary 22

Internet Sites 23

Index 24

Tall Tales

*T*here is a place in Wyoming where the earth steams. Fountains spout hot water. Gray, pink, white, and yellow mud holes bubble in the ground. Sound like a tall tale to you?

To people in the early 1800s it sounded like a made up story. Early Yellowstone **explorers** were laughed at when they told people what they saw. People thought they were crazy.

After a while, more explorers came back with the same stories. People soon realized that the explorers were not telling tales. The land of **thermal** wonders did exist.

In 1872, the area was set aside as Yellowstone National Park. Two million people visit the park each year. Listen to what they have to say. But don't believe everything you hear—Yellowstone has inspired many stories. One famous tall tale goes like this:

"Birds drink a lot of water from the **hot springs**. They drink so much that they lay hard boiled eggs."

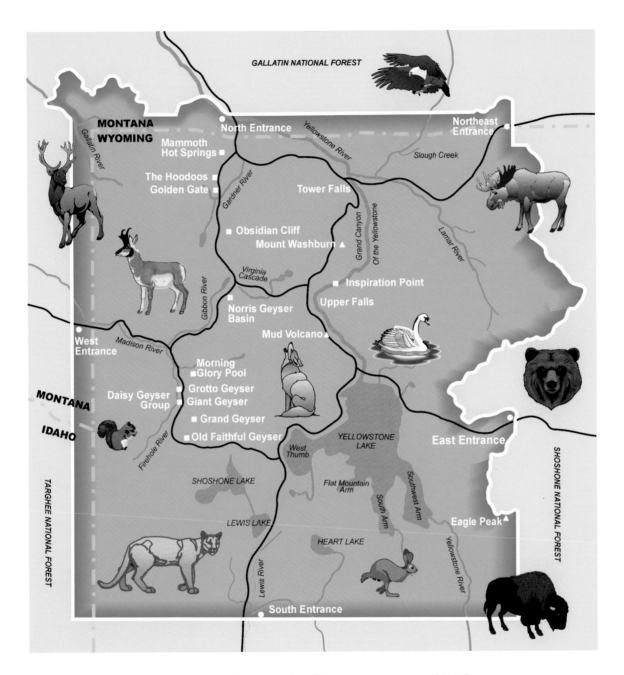

An illustrated map of Yellowstone National Park.

The First National Park

*I*n 1872, President Ulysses S. Grant signed a bill making Yellowstone the world's first national park. Today there are about 1200 national parks around the world. The purpose of national parks is to **preserve** nature. In national parks hunting, mining, grazing, and logging are not allowed.

In 1872, people had never heard of a national park. There were a lot of questions. What's the best way to run a park? What's the best way to show people the animals, **geysers**, and **hot springs**? What's the best way to protect nature?

When Yellowstone first opened, some people hunted the buffalo. The number of buffalo in the park quickly dropped. Today, park officials make sure that people do not hunt. Buffalo numbers are back up.

Over the years, some ideas about Yellowstone have worked. Some ideas have failed. There are no simple answers. As time goes on, we will continue to learn how to better protect our national parks.

The Boiling River, a popular swimming area near the Mammoth Hot Springs.

Glaciers and Volcanoes

*Y*ellowstone National Park is over two million acres of natural beauty. There are tall mountains and deep canyons. A river, swimming with life, winds through the park.

What you see today was not always there. Long ago, **glaciers** and volcanoes formed Yellowstone's **landscape**.

A glacier is a huge mass of snow and ice. As a glacier melts, it slides. Sliding glaciers carved deep canyons and filled lakes and rivers with water in Yellowstone.

Deep in the earth there is a layer of melted rock. The melted rock is called magma. Sometimes the magma **erupts** on the earth's surface through a hole called a volcano. When magma erupts on the surface, it is called **lava**. When lava cools, it hardens into rock.

If the volcano spews a lot of lava, mountains are formed. Many of the mountains at Yellowstone were created by ancient volcanoes.

The Mammoth Hot Springs in winter.

Hot Springs and Mud Pots

*T*he land under Yellowstone is very hot. The land is so hot that it causes **hot springs**, **mud pots**, and **geysers** to form. Some hot springs are over 400° Fahrenheit (204° Celsius)!

As the land grows hotter, water that is trapped underground heats up. The water expands and turns to steam. The force of the steam is so great that it searches for a place to get out. A hot spring is formed when the steam pushes up into a pool of water. The most famous hot spring is Morning Glory Pool.

A mud pot is created when the steam comes up through a mud puddle. If you hear a glugging sound, look around. You may be near a mud pot. They make funny sounds.

There are many different colors in hot springs and mud pots. The colors in mud pots and hot springs are created by **bacteria** and **algae**.

A hot spring in Yellowstone National Park.

Geysers

A **geyser** is a special kind of **hot spring**. A geyser is a hot spring with a huge amount of water and steam trapped underground. When the water and steam can no longer be held inside the earth, they **erupt** through a hole in the ground. The force behind a geyser is much greater than the force behind a regular hot spring.

Different geysers spew different amounts of water and steam. The tallest geyser in Yellowstone erupts water to a height of up to 380 feet (116 m)!

Some geysers erupt for a few minutes. Some erupt for only seconds. The eruption stops when the geyser has run out of energy (the force pushing the water out) or when the geyser has run out of water.

Some geysers, like Old Faithful, erupt at regular times. Other geysers erupt once a year or less. How often and how much a geyser erupts depends on how much water and energy lie below its surface.

This geyser, named Old Faithful, is erupting high into the air.

Wildlife

*Y*ellowstone National Park is home to many animals. Grizzly bears, black bears, moose, pronghorn, coyote, bighorn sheep, and cougars live in the park. Other animals do, too.

Visitors often spot buffaloes, elk, and bears. Keep your distance! Wild animals are dangerous. Cute baby bears have very sharp claws. A mama bear's claws are even sharper. And she is much bigger!

Even if you do not see any animals, you can often hear them. During mating season male bighorn sheep charge at each other. Their horns slam together. The fight is so loud it can be heard from far away.

More than 250 types of birds live in the park. Trumpeter swans, blue herons, bald eagles, gulls, and pelicans are a few of the birds that nest in Yellowstone. They eat the fish that swim in Yellowstone's lakes and rivers.

A red fox in Yellowstone National Park.

Plant Life

*T*here are many kinds of trees and plants in Yellowstone. The most common tree is the lodgepole pine. The lodgepole pine is a straight, tall tree that can grow up to 75 feet (23 m).

Hundreds of years ago, Native Americans made lodgepole pine trees into beams for their lodges. That's how the lodgepole got its name.

Douglas fir, limber pine, and Engelmann spruce are also found in Yellowstone's forests.

In the summer beautiful wild flowers cover the mountains and meadows. The fairy slipper is a type of orchid that looks like a little slipper.

The yellow monkey flower grows in wet areas. If you look closely at the flower, you will see that it looks like a monkey's face.

Wyoming paintbrush, lupine, mountain bluebell, and fringed gentian also add beautiful colors to Yellowstone's **landscape**.

16

Lodgepole pines in Yellowstone National Park.

Fun Things to Do

*T*here are many fun things to do at Yellowstone National Park. You can hike. You can camp. You can fish. You can even ride in a stage coach!

You can watch steam and water bubble and burst from the earth. **Hot springs**, **geysers**, and **mud pots** are found all over the park.

You can see a big mountain of black glass. The mountain is made of **obsidian**, a rock formed by hardened **lava**.

You can see **petrified** trees. About 50 million years ago ash and mud from volcanic **eruptions** buried the trees. The minerals from mud and water turned the trees into stone.

From June through Labor Day, Yellowstone has a special Junior Ranger program just for kids. Stop by a visitor center and ask how you can become a Junior Ranger. You may be able to earn a Junior Ranger patch!

There are thousands of things to see and do. Yellowstone National Park is waiting for you!

Winter hiking in Yellowstone National Park.

Help Preserve Yellowstone

*N*ature is very **fragile**. Without preserving natural habitats like Yellowstone, many native plants and animals would die.

Preserving Yellowstone is very important. You can help. When visiting Yellowstone follow these rules:

• Do not litter. Bring a small bag with you. Put your trash in your bag and bring it back out of the park. Pick up trash that you see on the ground and add that to your bag.

• Stay on the trails. This is for your own safety. Staying on the trails will **preserve** the rest of Yellowstone's land.

• Don't feed the animals. Animals need to find their own food. If they take your handouts, they may forget how to get their own food. When visitors stop coming at the end of the summer, the animals could starve.

Help to preserve Yellowstone's beauty by following the rules.

Glossary

Algae: a type of plant, mostly found in water. Algae can be anything from pond scum to seaweed.

Bacteria: small living things that can only be seen with a microscope.

Erupt: to explode and spurt all over.

Explorers: people who travel to new places.

Fragile: easily damaged.

Geyser: a natural hot-water fountain.

Glacier: a huge mass of snow and ice.

Hot spring: a hot pool of water created when pressurized steam rises up through surface water.

Landscape: the scenery of a land area.

Lava: melted rock that comes from a volcano.

Mud pot: a bubbling mud hole created when steam rises up through puddles of mud.

Obsidian: glass-like rock formed when lava cools.

Petrified: turned into stone.

Preserve: to keep safe and undisturbed.

Thermal: caused by heat.

Internet Sites

Canadian CultureNet
http://www.culturenet.ucalgary.ca/
CultureNet is a World Wide Web window on Canadian culture. It is a home for Canadian cultural networks.

The Disney World Explorer
http://www.disney.com/DisneyInteractive/WDWExplorer/
This is a fun and colorful site with trivia games, maps, previews, downloads, CD-ROM helpers and much, much more.

Grand Canyon Association
http://www.thecanyon.com/gca/
You're just a click away from a backpacking trip, a chance to meet canyon lovers like you, and books on this great region. This site has some great artwork.

Mexconnect
http://www.mexconnect.com/
This site has great travel ideas, Mexican art, tradition, food, history, and much more. It includes a chat room, tour section, and photo gallery.

Fantastic Journeys Yellowstone
http://www.nationalgeographic.com/features/97/yellowstone/index.html
Explore Yellowstone National Park, a place like no other on Earth. See strange marvels, go underground to find what causes them, and trigger an eruption of the famous geyser Old Faithful. A very cool site!

Marine Watch
http://www.marinewatch.com/
Welcome to Marine Watch, the international news journal about events occurring on, under and over the oceans of the planet. This site has many links and cool photos!

These sites are subject to change.

Pass It On

Adventure Enthusiasts: Tell us about places you've been or want to see. A national park, amusement park, or any exciting place you want to tell us about. We want to hear from you!

To get posted on the ABDO Publishing Company website E-mail us at
"Adventure@abdopub.com"
Visit the ABDO Publishing Company website at www.abdopub.com

Index

A

animals 6, 14, 20

B

bears 14
birds 4, 14
buffalo 6, 14

C

camp 18
canyons 8

E

eagles 14
elk 14
eruptions 18
explorers 4

F

fish 14, 18
flowers 16
forests 16
fountains 4

G

geysers 6, 10, 12, 18
glaciers 8
Grant, Ulysses S. 6

H

hike 18
hot springs 4, 6, 10, 12, 18
hunting 6

J

Junior Ranger program 18

L

landscape 8, 16
lava 8, 18
litter 20
logging 6

M

minerals 18
mining 6
moose 14
Morning Glory Pool 10
mountains 8, 16, 18
mud pots 10, 18

N

national parks 6
Native Americans 16

O

Old Faithful 12

P

plants 16, 20
preserving Yellowstone 20

R

river 8, 14

S

sheep 14

T

trails 20
trees 16, 18

V

volcanoes 8

W

Wyoming 4, 16